# Love My First S...

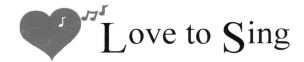 Love to Sing

*Love My First Songbook is for you Debs.*

*"May the music of life fill your soul with joy - everyday!"*

**Thank you SO much Janice Robinson and the children from Elm Park Primary School:**
*Loryn Bennett, David Cory-Toussant, Lucy Doige, Julia Flack, Carolyn Jentzsch, Louise Mansfield, Libby Paget, Angela Rowe, Anita Thi, Mariam Viray, and Jamie White.*

**Special thanks for your support and help:**
*Jamie-Lee and Tessa Adamson, my family especially Harry Jekel, David Daniel, Chris Little, Stephen Seth and Debbie Vaughan.*

*Love My First Songbook was first published in September 1996 by Love to Sing, © Linda Adamson.*

*Love My First Songbook (with Tape) ISBN 0-958-3563-1-9*
*Love My First Songbook (with CD) ISBN 0-958-3563-2-7*

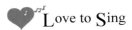Love to Sing

*PO Box 11 415, Ellerslie, Auckland, New Zealand.*

*Produced by:* **Linda Adamson**
*Musical Arrangements by:* **Brent Holt**
*Synthesizer Programming by:* **Brent Holt**
*Recorded at:* **KB Studio, Maraetai**
*Sound Engineers:* **Brent Holt & David Walker**
*Pre-press Production:* **Jonathan Guthrie**
*Printing:* **Theo Visser**

*Music © **Copyright clearance via AMCOS***

**Other Titles by Linda Adamson:**
*Love to Sing and Dance (with Tape or CD) Love to Sing*
*Love to Sing Christmas Songs (with Tape or CD) Love to Sing*
*Love My Times Tables (with Tape, wipe off cards and pen) Love to Sing*
also:  *Love to Learn Songbook (with Tape) Scholastic NZ Ltd*
    *Love to Sing Nursery Rhymes (with Tape) Scholastic NZ Ltd*
*All of the above are © Linda Adamson*

# CONTENTS

# 1. Hey Baby Let's Rock and Roll

Hey baby, hey baby let's rock and roll [G]
Hey baby, hey baby let's rock and roll [C] [G]

We're gonna jump, jump, turn around [G]
We're gonna twist, twist, to the ground [C] [A7]
Hey baby let's rock and roll [G] [D7] [G]

Hey baby, hey baby let's rock and roll [G]
Hey baby, hey baby let's rock and roll [C] [G]

We're gonna twirl, twirl, way up high [G]
We're gonna shake, shake, to the sky [C] [A7]
Hey baby let's rock and roll [G] [D7] [G]

*Repeat*

*"Rock and roll" to the music.*

*Dance the actions suggested by the words.*

4

# 2. Jack in the Box

**Chorus:**

Jack in the box, Jack in the box *(E)*
Quiet and still *(F#m)*
Will you come out? Will you come out? *(B)*
Yes I will! *(B)* *(E)*
What can you do? *(B)* *(E)* *(B7)*

My hands are shaking, shaking, shaking *(E)* *(F#m)* *(E)*
My hands are shaking just like this *(E)* *(F#m)* *(B)* *(E)*

**Repeat Chorus**

My head is nodding, nodding, nodding
My head is nodding just like this

**Repeat Chorus**

My eyes are blinking, blinking, blinking
My eyes are blinking just like this

**Repeat Chorus**

My feet are stamping, stamping, stamping
My feet are stamping just like this

**Repeat Chorus**

My hands are clapping, clapping, clapping
My hands are clapping just like this

*Form a circle, chosen child is in the centre.*

*Crouch down low*

*Index finger on lips*

*Hold out hands*

*Jump up high*

*Hold out hands.*

*Shake hands in time to the music.*

*"Jack" chooses a new "Jack" at the end of each verse.*

*Nod head in time to the music.*

*Blink eyes in time to the music.*

*Stamp feet in time to the music.*

*Clap hands in time to the music.*

# 3. Five Little Speckled Frogs

Five little speckled frogs sitting upon a log
<sub>A</sub> <sub>D</sub>
Eating a most delicious bug, yum, yum!
<sub>A</sub> <sub>E</sub>
One jumped into the pool where it was nice and cool
<sub>A</sub>
Then there were four green speckled frogs
<sub>E</sub> <sub>A</sub>

Four little speckled frogs...

Three little speckled frogs...

Two little speckled frogs...

One little speckled frog sitting upon a log
Eating a most delicious bug, yum, yum!
He jumped into the pool where it was nice and cool
Then there were no green speckled frogs

*A wonderful song to play act to.*

*Characters required:*
*Five little speckled frogs.*

*Alternatively use "fingers" to represent*
*the frogs.*

# 4. I Love to March

I love to march
I love to march
I love to march
To the beat of the drum

I love to march
I love to march
I love to march
To the slide of the trombone

I love to march
I love to march
I love to march
To the crash of the cymbals

I love to march
I love to march
I love to march
To the sound of the band

*A great marching song!*
*March in time to the music.*

*Beat your "pretend" drum.*

*March in time to the music.*

*Slide your "pretend" trombone.*

*March in time to the music.*

*Crash your "pretend" cymbals.*

*March in time to the music.*

*Do all the above instrument actions.*

# 5. Where is Thumbkin?

Where is thumbkin? Where is thumbkin?
Here I am, here I am
How are you this morning?
Very well I thank you
Run away, run away

Where is pointer? ...

Where is tallman? ...

Where is ringman? ...

Where is pinkie? ...

Where is everyone? Where is everyone?
Here we are, here we are
How are you this morning?
Very well we thank you
Run away, run away

*Place hands behind your back*

*Bring out right thumb, bring out left thumb*

*Face thumbs together, wriggle right thumb,*

*Wriggle left thumb.*

*Right thumb behind back, left thumb behind back.*

*Use appropriate fingers to show the actions.*

# 6. Little Peter Rabbit

Little Peter Rabbit had a fly upon his nose (E, A)
Little Peter Rabbit had a fly upon his nose (E)
Little Peter Rabbit had a fly upon his nose (C#m)
So he flipped it and he flopped it, but it wouldn't go away (F#m, B7, E)

*Chorus:*     Poor little Peter Rabbit (E)
            Poor little Peter Rabbit (A, E)
            Poor little Peter Rabbit (E, C#m)
            So he flipped it and he flopped it, (F#m, B7)
                but it wouldn't go away (E)

Little Peter Rabbit had a butterfly on his chin (x3)
So he shooed it and he shooed it, but it wouldn't go away

*Chorus:*     Poor little Peter Rabbit (x3)
            So he shooed it and he shooed it,
                but it wouldn't go away

Little Peter Rabbit had a spider on his knee (x3)
So he flicked it and he flicked it, but it wouldn't go away

*Chorus:*     Poor little Peter Rabbit (x3)
            So he flicked it and he flicked it,
                but it wouldn't go away

Little Peter Rabbit had an elephant on his toe (x3)
So he pushed it and he pushed it, but it wouldn't go away

*Chorus:*     Poor little Peter Rabbit (x3)
            So he pushed it and he pushed it,
                but it wouldn't go away

*Mime the actions suggested by the words.*

# 7. The Mulberry Bush

**Chorus:** Here we go round the mulberry bush *(Eb)*
The mulberry bush, *(Bb)* the mulberry bush *(Eb)*
Here we go round the mulberry bush *(Eb)*
On a cold *(Bb)* and frosty morning *(Eb)*

*Hold hands to form a circle and dance around.*

This is the way we wash our face, *(Eb)*
Wash our face, *(Bb)* wash our face, *(Eb)*
This is the way we wash our face, *(Eb)*
On a cold *(Bb)* and frosty morning *(Eb)*

*Stand still and perform the actions.*

***Repeat Chorus***

This is the way we comb our hair...

***Repeat Chorus***

This is the way we brush our teeth...

***Repeat Chorus***

This is the way we put on our clothes...

***Repeat Chorus***

# 8. The Wheels on the Bus

* The wheels on the bus go round and round
Round and round, round and round
The wheels on the bus go round and round
All around the town

*Twirl hands round each other*

*Spread arms out to form a big circle.*

The wipers on the bus go swish, swish, swish...

*Keep palms together and sway hands side to side.*

The horn on the bus goes beep, beep, beep...

*"Honk" nose with index finger.*

The doors on the bus go open and shut...

*Big hand claps*

The babies on the bus go "Boo hoo hoo"...

*Show sad face and wipe away "pretend" tears*

The driver of the bus says "Please sit down"...

*Shake index finger, place other hand on hip.*

*Repeat*

18

# 9. Teddy Bear Medley

* Round and round the garden <sub>C</sub>
  Went the Teddy Bear <sub>F</sub>
  One step, <sub>G</sub>
  Two steps,
  Tickley under there <sub>C</sub>

Teddy Bear, Teddy Bear, turn around
Teddy Bear, Teddy Bear, touch the ground
Teddy Bear, Teddy Bear, point to the sky
Teddy Bear, Teddy Bear, try to fly
Teddy Bear, Teddy Bear, peek a boo
Teddy Bear, Teddy Bear, skiddle skaddle doo

Teddy Bear, Teddy Bear, prance, prance, prance
Teddy Bear, Teddy Bear, kick and dance
Teddy Bear, Teddy Bear, point your toe
Teddy Bear, Teddy Bear, hop just so
Teddy Bear, Teddy Bear, peek a boo
Teddy Bear, Teddy Bear, skiddle skaddle doo

* Repeat

*With your index finger "draw" circles on child's palm.*

*"Jump" your index finger up childs arm*

*Tickle the child under the arm.*

*Show the actions as suggested by the words.*

# 10. On the Farm

On the farm there lives a cow
(D) (A)
And that cow she gives us milk
(A) (D)
Milk to drink!

On the farm there lives a hen
And that hen she lays an egg
I like it boiled!

On the farm there lives a cat
And that cat can catch a rat
Fancy that!

On the farm there lives a horse
And that horse takes us for rides
It's fun of course!

On the farm there lives a sheep
And that sheep she gives us wool
It keeps me warm!

On the farm there lives a pig
And that pig makes grunting sounds
And mucks around!

On the farms there lives a dog
And that dog rounds up the sheep
Sure saves my feet!

*Have fun with appropriate animal sounds!*

on the farm there lives a cow

# 11. Fuzzy Wuzzy Caterpillar

Fuzzy wuzzy caterpillar humps along
Humps along, humps along
Fuzzy, wuzzy caterpillar humps along
Out to see the world

*Wriggle hand and arm up and down.*

*Spread arms out to form a big circle.*

Fuzzy wuzzy caterpillar goes to sleep
Goes to sleep, goes to sleep
Fuzzy, wuzzy caterpillar goes to sleep
In his warm cocoon

*Rest head on hands.*

*Wrap arms around yourself.*

Someday you will be a pretty butterfly
Butterfly, butterfly
Someday you will be a pretty butterfly
Out to see the world

*Flap both arms out.*

*Spread arms out to form a big circle.*

# 12. This is the Way the Lady Rides

This is the way the lady rides
Trit, trot, trit, trot
This is the way the lady rides
Trit, trit, trot

This is the way the gentleman rides
Trit-trot, trit-trot, trit-trot, trit-trot
This is the way the gentleman rides
Trit-trot, trit-trot, trit-trot

This is the way the farmer rides
Gall-op, gall-op, gall-op, gall-op
This is the way the farmer rides
Gall-op, gall-op, gall-op

This is the way the old man rides
Hobble-dy, hobble-dy, hobble-dy
This is the way the old man rides
And down into the ditch!

*A great knee riding song!*

*Older children can ride a "pretend horse" to the beat of the rhyme.*

*Holding the baby, let him/her "fall" between your knees.*

# 13. Five Little Ducks

Five little ducks went swimming one day
<sup>F</sup> <sup>C</sup>
Over the pond and far away
<sup>F</sup>
Mother said "Quack quack quack"
<sup>F</sup> <sup>C</sup>
But only four little ducks came back
<sup>F</sup>

Four little ducks went swimming one day...

Three little ducks went swimming one day...

Two little ducks went swimming one day...

One little duck went swimming one day
Over the pond and far away
Mother said "Quack quack quack"
But no little ducks came back

Mother duck said "QUACK QUACK QUACK"
And all her five little ducks came back!

*A wonderful song to play act to.*

**Characters required:**
*Five little ducks,*
*A mother duck.*

*Alternatively use fingers to represent little ducks and wiggle them over your shoulder. Your other hand represents the mother duck and when she says, "Quack, quack, quack", open and close fingers on your thumb. Repeat using the correct amount of fingers as suggested by the words.*

# 14. Open, Shut Them

Open, shut them, open, shut them
[Db] [Ab] [Db] [Ab]
Give a little clap
[Db] [Ab]
Open, shut them, open, shut them
[Db] [Ab]
Lay them in your lap
[Gb] [Ab] [Db]

Creep them, creep them, creep them, creep them
Right up to your chin
Open wide your little mouth
But do not put them in

Roll them, roll them, roll them, roll them
Roll them just like this
Shake them, shake them, shake them, shake them
Blow a little kiss

Build them, build them, build them, build them
Make a little house
Tip toe, tip toe, tip toe, tip toe
Do not wake the mouse

Flying, flying, flying, flying
Up into the sky
Soaring, soaring, soaring, soaring
Through the clouds so high

Waving, waving, waving, waving
Bye to one and all
Swaying, swaying, swaying, swaying
Farewell to you all

*Using both hands, show the actions suggested by the words.*

**30**

# 15. Feelings, Feelings

**Chorus:**  
     Feelings, feelings <sub>D</sub>  
     They're a part of me <sub>G</sub> <sub>A</sub>  
     Feelings, feelings  
     I just want to be me. <sub>D</sub>

*Sit down in a circle*  
*Cross arms and join hands*  
*Sway in time to the music.*

Oh I feel happy, I feel happy  
When you smile at me  
I feel happy, oh so happy  
When you smile at me

*Hug yourself*  
*Smile to each other.*

**Repeat Chorus**

Oh I feel safe, I feel safe  
When you hold my hand...

*Hug yourself*  
*Hold each other's hand.*

**Repeat Chorus**

Oh I feel proud, I feel proud  
When you say "well done"...

*Hug yourself*  
*Pat each other on the back.*

**Repeat Chorus**

Oh I feel loved, I feel loved  
When you give me a hug...

*Hug yourself*  
*Hug each other.*

**Repeat Chorus**

Oh I feel special, I feel special  
When you say "I love you"...

*Hug yourself*  
*Say "I love you" to each other.*

**Repeat Chorus**

# 16. Lullaby Medley

\* Twinkle, twinkle little star,
How I wonder what you are,
Up above the world so high,
Like a diamond in the sky.
Twinkle, twinkle, little star,
How I wonder what you are.

Sleep, baby, sleep, thy father tends the sheep
Thy mother rocks the slumber-tree
And softly falls a dream for thee
Sleep, baby, sleep.

Golden slumbers kiss your eyes
Smiles awake you when you rise
Sleep, pretty darling, do not cry,
And I will sing a lullaby.
Lullaby, lullaby, lullaby.

Care you know not, therefore sleep,
While I o'er you watch do keep.
Sleep pretty darling, do not cry,
And I will sing a lullaby.
Lullaby, lullaby, lullaby.

*Snuggle up close and gently sway to the music.*

*Sweet dreams!*

\# Lullaby, my pretty one
Gone the day and set the sun
Lullaby, my pretty one
And sleep until the morning
and sleep until the morning.

*# Repeat*

Rock-a-bye baby on the tree top
When the wind blows the cradle will rock
When the bough breaks the cradle will fall
And down will come baby, cradle and all.

*\* Repeat*

A message from the author...

# **Babies are born music lovers**

"Those that do teach young babes
Do it with gentle means and easy tasks."    (William Shakespeare)

Music truly is one of childhood's most rewarding experiences. Here's why:-

💜 Singing will help build warm and loving relationships with your child.

💜 Babies derive immense pleasure from hearing your voice and from the familiarity of your songs.

💜 In infancy babies use "singsong chants" to practice sounds and words.

💜 Singing and learning new songs builds self esteem.

💜 Repetition of songs helps to build memory skills.

💜 Fingerplays and action songs help to develop fine motor skills and gross motor co-ordination.

💜 Singing soothes babies and toddlers.

💜 Sing spontaneous "made-up" songs - it will awaken a child's humour!

💜 Singing together is FUN!

## Linda's motto:

"You do not need to be a musical expert to share singing and dancing with children. ENTHUSIASM is the key - hang loose and enjoy the experience - children will respond whole-heartedly!"

*Linda Adamson*